HIS NAME IS...

ALPHA AND OMEGA
BRIGHT MORNING STAR
GOOD SHEPHERD
PRINCE OF PEACE

AT LOVE GOD GREATLY, YOU'LL FIND REAL, AUTHENTIC WOMEN. WOMEN WHO ARE IMPERFECT, YET FORGIVEN.

Women who desire less of us, and a whole lot more of Jesus. Women who long to know God through his Word, because we know that Truth transforms and sets us free. Women who are better together, saturated in God's Word and in community with one another.

Welcome, friend. We're so glad you're here...

CONTENTS

WELCOME

We are glad you have decided to join us in this Bible study! First of all, please know that you have been prayed for! It is not a coincidence you are participating in this study.

Our prayer for you is simple: that you will grow closer to our Lord as you dig into His Word each and every day! As you develop the discipline of being in God's Word on a daily basis, our prayer is that you will fall in love with Him even more as you spend time reading from the Bible.

Each day before you read the assigned Scripture(s), pray and ask God to help you understand it. Invite Him to speak to you through His Word. Then listen. It's His job to speak to you, and it's your job to listen and obey.

Take time to read the verses over and over again. We are told in Proverbs to search and you will find: "Search for it like silver, and hunt for it like hidden treasure. Then you will understand" (Prov. 2:4–5 NCV).

All of us here at Love God Greatly can't wait for you to get started, and we hope to see you at the finish line. Endure, persevere, press on—and don't give up! Finish well what you are beginning today. We will be here every step of the way, cheering you on! We are in this together. Fight to rise early, to push back the stress of the day, to sit alone and spend time in God's Word! Let's see what God has in store for you in this study! Journey with us as we learn to love God greatly with our lives!

As you go through this study, join us in the following resources below:

Weekly Blog Posts •

Weekly Memory Verses •

Weekly Challenges •

Facebook, Twitter, Instagram •

LoveGodGreatly.com •

Hashtag: #LoveGodGreatly •

RESOURCES

Join Us

ONLINE

lovegodgreatly.com

STORE

lovegodgreatly.com/store

FACEBOOK

facebook.com/LoveGodGreatly

INSTAGRAM

instagram.com/lovegodgreatlyofficial

TWITTER

@_LoveGodGreatly

DOWNLOAD THE APP

CONTACT US

info@lovegodgreatly.com

CONNECT

#LoveGodGreatly

LOVE
GOD
GREATLY

Love God Greatly (LGG) is a beautiful community of women who use a variety of technology platforms to keep each other accountable in God's Word. We start with a simple Bible reading plan, but it doesn't stop there.

Some women gather in homes and churches locally, while others connect online with women across the globe. Whatever the method, we lovingly lock arms and unite for this purpose: to love God greatly with our lives.

Would you consider reaching out and doing this study with someone?

In today's fast-paced technology-driven world, it would be easy to study God's Word in an isolated environment that lacks encouragement or support, but that isn't the intention here at Love God Greatly. God created us to live in community with Him and with those around us.

We need each other, and we live life better together. Because of this, would you consider reaching out and doing this study with someone?

Rest assured we'll be studying right alongside you—learning with you, cheering for you, enjoying sweet fellowship, and smiling from ear to ear as we watch God unite women together—intentionally connecting hearts and minds for His glory.

So here's the challenge: call your mom, your sister, your grandma, the girl across the street, or the college friend across the country. Gather a group of girls from your church or workplace, or meet in a coffee shop with friends you have always wished you knew better.

Arm-in-arm and hand-in-hand, let's do this thing...together.

SOAP STUDY

HOW AND WHY TO SOAP

In this study we offer you a study journal to accompany the verses we are reading. This journal is designed to help you interact with God's Word and learn to dig deeper, encouraging you to slow down and reflect on what God is saying to you that day.

At Love God Greatly, we use the SOAP Bible study method. Before beginning, let's take a moment to define this method and share why we recommend using it during your quiet time in the following pages.

The most important ingredients in the Soap method are your interaction with God's Word and your application of His Word to your life.

It's one thing to simply read Scripture. But when you interact with it, intentionally slowing down to really reflect on it, suddenly words start popping off the page. The SOAP method allows you to dig deeper into Scripture and see more than you would if you simply read the verses and then went on your merry way.

The most important ingredients in the SOAP method are your interaction with God's Word and your application of His Word to your life:

Blessed is the one who does not walk in step with the wicked or stand in the way that sinners take or sit in the company of mockers, but whose delight is in the law of the LORD, and who meditates on his law day and night. That person is like a tree planted by streams of water, which yields its fruit in season and whose leaf does not wither—whatever they do prospers.
(Ps. 1:1–3, NIV)

Please take the time to SOAP through our Bible studies and see for yourself how much more you get from your daily reading.

You'll be amazed.

S STANDS FOR
SCRIPTURE

Physically write out the verses.

You'll be amazed at what God will reveal to you just by taking the time to slow down and write out what you are reading!

MONDAY

READ
Colossians 1:5–8

SOAP
Colossians 1:5–8

Scripture

WRITE
OUT THE
SCRIPTURE
PASSAGE
FOR THE
DAY

The faith and love that spring from the hope stored up for you in heaven and about which you have already heard in the true message of the gospel that has come to you. In the same way the gospel is bearing fruit and growing throughout the whole world just as it has been doing among you since the day you heard it and truly understood God's grace. You learned it from Epaphras, our dear fellow servant, who is a faithful minister of Christ on our behalf, and who also told us of your love in the Spirit.

Observations

WRITE
DOWN 1 OR 2
OBSERVATIONS
FROM THE
PASSAGE.

When you combine faith and love, you get hope. We must remember that our hope is in heaven; it is yet to come. The gospel is the Word of truth. The gospel is continually bearing fruit and growing from the first day to the last. It just takes one person to change a whole community. Epaphras.

O STANDS FOR
OBSERVATION

What do you see in the verses that you're reading?

Who is the intended audience? Is there a repetition of words?

What words stand out to you?

A STANDS FOR **APPLICATION**

This is when God's Word becomes personal.

What is God saying to you today?

How can you apply what you just read to your own personal life?

What changes do you need to make? Is there action you need to take?

Applications

WRITE DOWN 1 OR 2 APPLICATIONS FROM THE PASSAGE.

God used one man, Epaphras, to change a whole town. I was reminded that we are simply called to tell others about Christ; it's God's job to spread the gospel, to grow it, and have it bear fruit. I felt today's verses were almost directly spoken to Love God Greatly women: "The gospel is bearing fruit and growing throughout the whole world just as it has been doing among you since the day you heard it and truly understood God's grace.

Pray

WRITE OUT A PRAYER OVER WHAT YOU LEARNED FROM TODAY'S PASSAGE.

Dear Lord, please help me to be an Epaphras, to tell others about You and then leave the results in Your loving hands. Please help me to understand and apply personally what I have read today to my life, thereby becoming more and more like You each and every day. Help me to live a life that bears the fruit of faith and love, anchoring my hope in heaven, not here on earth. Help me to remember that the best is yet to come!

P STANDS FOR **PRAYER**

Pray God's Word back to Him. Spend time thanking Him.

If He has revealed something to you during this time in His Word, pray about it.

If He has revealed some sin that is in your life, confess. And remember, He loves you dearly.

A RECIPE FOR YOU

OMA'S (GRANDMA'S) VANILLE KIPFERL

These light and delicious cookies are made from ground almonds, and are flavored with vanilla and a coating of sugar. Be aware, there are only a few ingredients in a Vanille Kipferl cookie. This means that each ingredient is important. Don't substitute margarine for butter, and stay away from stale or old almonds. The correct, fresh flavors will beautifully shine through!

Yield: 50 Cookies

Ingredients

1 1/2 Cup (260g) flour

1 egg yolk

2 tsp. vanilla extract

3/4 Cup (80g) powdered sugar

1 Cup (100g) ground almonds

1 Cup (200g) cold butter, cubed

1/3 to 1/2 Cup vanilla sugar
(can be found on Amazon)

Directions

- Sieve the flour into a heap on a pastry board or into a large bowl.

- Cut the cold butter into small pieces and mix with the flour. Add powdered sugar, ground almonds or hazelnuts, vanilla extract, and the egg.

- Rinse hands with cold water and quickly knead mixture into a crisp dough. Chill for half an hour.

- Form thumb thick rolls from the dough, then cut into 1 inch wide pieces and roll to form crescents.

- Bake at 160° Celsius (320 Fahrenheit) for 10-15 minutes, or until very light gold in color.

- Turn the crescents in a mixture of powdered sugar and vanilla sugar while still hot. Enjoy!

LGG GERMAN TESTIMONY

EMILY, GERMANY

My name is Emily Dorn. I'm 35 years old and I've been married to my Kindergarten sweetheart for 15 years. We have three children (ages 8, 6, and 1) and we live in Frankfurt, Germany. I am one of two German translators and I've been serving with Love God Greatly for three and a half years now.

Or I should say, over three years ago – by the grace of God - Love God Greatly found me.

I was going through a very difficult season and was filled with pain and grief. Spending time in God's presence and in His Word wasn't easy for me. There was so much I didn't understand or want to hear at that time.

My sister - who is one of the writing contributors for LGG - told me that they were looking for a German translator and asked if I could step in just until they found someone permanently. I thought, "Sure, why not? That doesn't involve me having to communicate directly with God, right?!"

But let me tell you, with every study I translated and every word I typed, God was speaking straight to my hurting heart. My rough edges began to soften and it didn't take long before I was back to where God had intended for me to be all along.

Also, I never saw my bilingual upbringing as anything special or of any great use. Becoming a translator for LGG showed me how God can use even the "little things" to bring people...women... me... closer to Him!

I meet a lot of women and moms who are totally focused and maybe even a little overwhelmed with trying to be a good mother, wife, friend, or coworker. They feel burdened with guilt because they hardly make the time to read God's Word. LGG blesses them

Or I should say, over three years ago – by the grace of God – Love God Greatly found me.

so much because of the way the material is set up. It helps them get into God's Word simply and relationally. They feel supported and encouraged, but they are also given the space needed for personal reflection and quiet time with the Lord. I think the combination of Bible study and journaling is a great way to help them process their thoughts and keep them grounded when life gets busy and demanding again.

LGG is a blessing for German speaking countries for so many reasons:

LGG Bible studies offer German speaking women a different way of "doing faith" that is still uncommon in Christian circles here.

The group dynamic that is part of LGG brings a life-giving challenge to German speaking women to move deeper into relationship with one another. This biblical model helps them to be more authentic and build stronger bonds with each other.

The SOAP method gives them a framework to follow and invites them to dig deeper into Scripture. The study questions offer some topics to think about and discuss.

The online presence of LGG material is helpful because it makes it easy to access and share with others. This is attractive to those living in progressive countries.

What German speaking women are saying about LGG...

Silja from Munich: LGG enables me to keep a more regular routine of reading Scripture, especially when times get stressful and difficult. The material is thought provoking and makes God's Word come to life in my everyday routines.

Barbara from Switzerland: LGG is a huge answer to a silent prayer. I want to share my heartfelt thanks for the encouragement I have received and for the opportunity to build bridges by connecting with a LGG group.

Andrea from Frankfurt: I still feel a little insecure and overwhelmed when reading the Bible on my own. LGG takes me by the hand and leads me into God's Word in a very simple way. The selected Bible verses and corresponding reflection questions help me see things clearly and in ways I might not have figured out on my own.

To connect with LGG German Branch:

• facebook.com/LoveGodGreatlyDeutsch

Do you know someone who could use our Love God Greatly Bible studies in German? If so, make sure and tell them about LGG German and all the amazing Bible study resources we provide to help equip them with God's Word!!!

HIS NAME IS...

ALPHA AND OMEGA

BRIGHT MORNING STAR

GOOD SHEPHERD

PRINCE OF PEACE

Let's Begin

INTRODUCTION

"Therefore God exalted Him to the highest place and gave Him the name that is above every name..."
- Philippians 2:9

The story of redemption begins in the first book of the Bible. In the early part of Genesis, after Adam and Eve had disobeyed God through the temptation of the serpent, God promised that a Redeemer would come who would crush the head of that serpent (Genesis 3). This was the first offering of the "good news" of God's saving grace. As the years went by, God meticulously arranged people and events in such a way that brought about the coming of this serpent crusher.

When the time was right God united two ordinary people, Mary and Joseph, who would become the last pieces of the redemption puzzle. When these two were betrothed, an angel came and announced that God was about to take on flesh and become like the ones who needed salvation (Luke 1). This angel gave very specific instruction as to the name this child must have.

"Joseph, son of David, do not fear to take Mary as your wife, for that which is conceived in her is from the Holy Spirit. She will bear a son, and you shall call His name Jesus, for He will save His people from their sins." - Matthew 1:20-21

Jesus—for He will save His people.
This name should be the most precious of names to us. In this name we are forgiven of sin and reconciled to God.

Throughout the Scriptures we see the importance of names. Names often say something about a person's character. Take Jacob, for example, whose name means "deceiver". Other times a name reflects a person's calling, like when Abram's name was changed to Abraham, meaning "the father of nations".

When it comes to God, one name just isn't adequate enough to tell of His great character and mighty power. **One name simply cannot contain our Savior.**

This Christmas season, join us as we look at four names that reveal to us the greatness of Jesus.

His name is...

The Alpha and Omega. Though Jesus was born like all humans are born, He actually has no beginning or end. He is the One in whom all things have their beginning and their ending.

The Bright Morning Star. The Christmas star guided the wise men to the Savior of the nations, but it is Jesus Himself who is our Bright Morning Star, who guides us to the Kingdom of God where we may find value, life, and freedom from sin.

The Good Shepherd. The job of a shepherd was hard. You had to be watchful and you had to be willing to risk your life for the sheep. Jesus is the Great Shepherd. His care for His people is constant. He not only watches over His sheep continually, but He went so far as to give His life so His sheep would be safe.

The Prince of Peace. In the world and in our own hearts, peace is not something that is found very easily. When we do seem to have a measure of it, it can be unstable and easily lost. But Jesus tells us that He is the Prince of Peace. In Him we can possess a peace that surpasses all understanding (Phil. 4:7).

Our prayer is that this Christmas you will look deeper into the person of Jesus through a closer examination of His names. May God cause us to grow in faith and adoration through a true knowledge of His Son.

READING PLAN

WEEK 1
The Bright Morning Star

Monday
READ - REVELATION 22:16
SOAP - REVELATION 22:16

Tuesday
READ - NUMBERS 24:15-17
SOAP - NUMBERS 24:17

Wednesday
READ - JOHN 8:12
SOAP - JOHN 8:12

Thursday
READ - 2 PETER 1:16-21
SOAP - 2 PETER 1:19

Friday
READ - MATTHEW 2:1-12
SOAP - MATTHEW 2:1-2, 10-11

WEEK 2
Alpha and Omega

Monday
READ - REVELATION 1:8; 22:13
SOAP - REVELATION 1:8

Tuesday
READ - COLOSSIANS 1:15-20
SOAP - COLOSSIANS 1:15, 17

Wednesday
READ - GENESIS 1:1; PSALM 90:2; JOHN 1:1
SOAP - PSALM 90:2

Thursday
READ - ISAIAH 44:6-8
SOAP - ISAIAH 44:6

Friday
READ - REVELATION 21:1-8
SOAP - REVELATION 21:4-8

WEEK 3
Good Shepherd

Monday
READ - JOHN 10:11-14
SOAP - JOHN 10:11, 14

Tuesday
READ - 1 PETER 2:24-25
SOAP - 1 PETER 2:25

Wednesday
READ - PSALM 23
SOAP - PSALM 23:1-3

Thursday
READ - PSALM 100
SOAP - PSALM 100:3

Friday
READ - LUKE 2:8-20; ISAIAH 40:11
SOAP - LUKE 2:8-11; ISAIAH 40:11

WEEK 4
Prince of Peace

Monday
READ - ISAIAH 9:6-7
SOAP - ISAIAH 9:6

Tuesday
READ - JOHN 14:27
SOAP - JOHN 14:27

Wednesday
READ - COLOSSIANS 3:15
SOAP - COLOSSIANS 3:15

Thursday
READ - JOHN 16:25-33
SOAP - JOHN 16:33

Friday
READ - ISAIAH 53:4-6
SOAP - ISAIAH 53:5

YOUR GOALS

We believe it's important to write out goals for this study. Take some time now and write three goals you would like to focus on as you begin to rise each day and dig into God's Word. Make sure and refer back to these goals throughout the next four weeks to help you stay focused. You can do it!

1.

2.

3.

Signature:

Date:

WEEK 1

The Bright Morning Star

I, Jesus, have sent my angel to testify to you about these things for the churches. I am the root and the descendant of David, the bright morning star.

REVELATION 22:16

PRAYER

Prayer focus for this week:
Spend time praying for your family members.

MONDAY

TUESDAY

WEDNESDAY

THURSDAY

FRIDAY

CHALLENGE

You can find this listed in our Monday blog post.

MONDAY
Scripture for Week 1

Revelation 22:16

16"I, Jesus, have sent my angel to testify to you about these
things for the churches. I am the root and the descendant of
David, the bright morning star."

MONDAY

READ:
Revelation 22:16

SOAP:
Revelation 22:16

Scripture

WRITE
OUT THE
SCRIPTURE
PASSAGE
FOR THE
DAY.

Observations

WRITE
DOWN 1 OR 2
OBSERVATIONS
FROM THE
PASSAGE.

Applications

WRITE
DOWN 1 OR 2
APPLICATIONS
FROM THE
PASSAGE.

Pray

WRITE OUT
A PRAYER
OVER WHAT
YOU LEARNED
FROM TODAY'S
PASSAGE.

TUESDAY

Scripture for Week 1

Numbers 24:15-17

15 And he took up his discourse and said,

"The oracle of Balaam the son of Beor,

    the oracle of the man whose eye is opened,

16 the oracle of him who hears the words of God,

    and knows the knowledge of the Most High,

who sees the vision of the Almighty,

    falling down with his eyes uncovered:

17 I see him, but not now;

    I behold him, but not near:

a star shall come out of Jacob,

    and a scepter shall rise out of Israel;

it shall crush the forehead of Moab

    and break down all the sons of Sheth.

TUESDAY

READ:
Numbers 24:15-17

SOAP:
Numbers 24:17

Scripture

WRITE
OUT THE
SCRIPTURE
PASSAGE
FOR THE
DAY.

Observations

WRITE
DOWN 1 OR 2
OBSERVATIONS
FROM THE
PASSAGE.

Applications

WRITE
DOWN 1 OR 2
APPLICATIONS
FROM THE
PASSAGE.

Pray

WRITE OUT
A PRAYER
OVER WHAT
YOU LEARNED
FROM TODAY'S
PASSAGE.

WEDNESDAY
Scripture for Week 1

John 8:12

12 Again Jesus spoke to them, saying, "I am the light of the world. Whoever follows me will not walk in darkness, but will have the light of life."

WEDNESDAY

READ:
John 8:12

SOAP:
John 8:12

Scripture

WRITE
OUT THE
SCRIPTURE
PASSAGE
FOR THE
DAY.

Observations

WRITE
DOWN 1 OR 2
OBSERVATIONS
FROM THE
PASSAGE.

Applications

WRITE
DOWN 1 OR 2
APPLICATIONS
FROM THE
PASSAGE.

Pray

WRITE OUT
A PRAYER
OVER WHAT
YOU LEARNED
FROM TODAY'S
PASSAGE.

THURSDAY
Scripture for Week 1

2 Peter 1:16-21

16 For we did not follow cleverly devised myths when we
made known to you the power and coming of our Lord
Jesus Christ, but we were eyewitnesses of his majesty. 17 For
when he received honor and glory from God the Father, and
the voice was borne to him by the Majestic Glory, "This
is my beloved Son, with whom I am well pleased," 18 we
ourselves heard this very voice borne from heaven, for
we were with him on the holy mountain. 19 And we
have the prophetic word more fully confirmed, to which
you will do well to pay attention as to a lamp shining
in a dark place, until the day dawns and the morning
star rises in your hearts, 20 knowing this first of all, that
no prophecy of Scripture comes from someone's own
interpretation. 21 For no prophecy was ever produced by the
will of man, but men spoke from God as they were carried
along by the Holy Spirit.

THURSDAY

READ:
2 Peter 1:16-21

SOAP:
2 Peter 1:19

Scripture

WRITE
OUT THE
SCRIPTURE
PASSAGE
FOR THE
DAY.

Observations

WRITE
DOWN 1 OR 2
OBSERVATIONS
FROM THE
PASSAGE.

Applications

WRITE
DOWN 1 OR 2
APPLICATIONS
FROM THE
PASSAGE.

Pray

WRITE OUT
A PRAYER
OVER WHAT
YOU LEARNED
FROM TODAY'S
PASSAGE.

FRIDAY
Scripture for Week 1

Matthew 2:1-12

1 Now after Jesus was born in Bethlehem of Judea in the
days of Herod the king, behold, wise men from the east
came to Jerusalem, 2 saying, "Where is he who has been
born king of the Jews? For we saw his star when it rose and
have come to worship him." 3 When Herod the king heard
this, he was troubled, and all Jerusalem with him; 4 and
assembling all the chief priests and scribes of the people, he
inquired of them where the Christ was to be born. 5 They
told him, "In Bethlehem of Judea, for so it is written by the
prophet:

6 "'And you, O Bethlehem, in the land of Judah,

   are by no means least among the rulers of Judah;

for from you shall come a ruler

   who will shepherd my people Israel.'"

7 Then Herod summoned the wise men secretly
and ascertained from them what time the star had
appeared. 8 And he sent them to Bethlehem, saying, "Go
and search diligently for the child, and when you have
found him, bring me word, that I too may come and
worship him." 9 After listening to the king, they went on
their way. And behold, the star that they had seen when it
rose went before them until it came to rest over the place
where the child was. 10 When they saw the star, they
rejoiced exceedingly with great joy. 11 And going into
the house, they saw the child with Mary his mother, and
they fell down and worshiped him. Then, opening their
treasures, they offered him gifts, gold and frankincense
and myrrh. 12 And being warned in a dream not to return to
Herod, they departed to their own country by another way.

FRIDAY

READ:
Matthew 2:1-12

SOAP:
Matthew 2:1-2, 10-11

Scripture

WRITE
OUT THE
SCRIPTURE
PASSAGE
FOR THE
DAY.

Observations

WRITE
DOWN 1 OR 2
OBSERVATIONS
FROM THE
PASSAGE.

Applications

WRITE
DOWN 1 OR 2
APPLICATIONS
FROM THE
PASSAGE.

Pray

WRITE OUT
A PRAYER
OVER WHAT
YOU LEARNED
FROM TODAY'S
PASSAGE.

REFLECTION
QUESTIONS

1. Why do you think Jesus is compared to a star?

2. Why are Christians called to be a light in the world?

3. How does following Jesus keep us out of darkness? What is the darkness?

4. What was the significance of the star that the wise men saw?

5. The star is something we use as a decoration at Christmas. How can we use the picture of the star to point our children, family, or friends to Jesus?

NOTES

WEEK 2

Alpha and Omega

---

*I am the Alpha and the Omega,"
says the Lord God, "who is and
who was and who is to come, the
Almighty."*

REVELATION 1:8

PRAYER

Prayer focus for this week:
Spend time praying for your country.

MONDAY

TUESDAY

WEDNESDAY

THURSDAY

FRIDAY

CHALLENGE

You can find this listed in our Monday blog post.

43

MONDAY
Scripture for Week 2

Revelation 1:8

8 "I am the Alpha and the Omega," says the Lord God, "who is and who was and who is to come, the Almighty."

Revelation 22:13
13 I am the Alpha and the Omega, the first and the last, the beginning and the end."

MONDAY

READ:
Revelation 1:8; 22:13

SOAP:
Revelation 1:8

Scripture

WRITE
OUT THE
SCRIPTURE
PASSAGE
FOR THE
DAY.

Observations

WRITE
DOWN 1 OR 2
OBSERVATIONS
FROM THE
PASSAGE.

Applications

WRITE
DOWN 1 OR 2
APPLICATIONS
FROM THE
PASSAGE.

Pray

WRITE OUT
A PRAYER
OVER WHAT
YOU LEARNED
FROM TODAY'S
PASSAGE.

TUESDAY

Scripture for Week 2

Colossians 1:15-20

15 He is the image of the invisible God, the firstborn
of all creation. 16 For by him all things were created, in
heaven and on earth, visible and invisible, whether thrones
or dominions or rulers or authorities—all things were
created through him and for him. 17 And he is before all
things, and in him all things hold together. 18 And he is
the head of the body, the church. He is the beginning, the
firstborn from the dead, that in everything he might be
preeminent. 19 For in him all the fullness of God was
pleased to dwell, 20 and through him to reconcile to himself
all things, whether on earth or in heaven, making peace by
the blood of his cross.

TUESDAY

READ:
Colossians 1:15-20

SOAP:
Colossians 1:15, 17

Scripture

WRITE
OUT THE
SCRIPTURE
PASSAGE
FOR THE
DAY.

Observations

WRITE
DOWN 1 OR 2
OBSERVATIONS
FROM THE
PASSAGE.

Applications

WRITE
DOWN 1 OR 2
APPLICATIONS
FROM THE
PASSAGE.

Pray

WRITE OUT
A PRAYER
OVER WHAT
YOU LEARNED
FROM TODAY'S
PASSAGE.

WEDNESDAY
Scripture for Week 2

Genesis 1:1

1 In the beginning, God created the heavens and the earth.

Psalm 90:2

2 Before the mountains were brought forth,

    or ever you had formed the earth and the world,

    from everlasting to everlasting you are God.

John 1:1

1 In the beginning was the Word, and the Word was with God, and the Word was God.

WEDNESDAY

READ:
Genesis 1:1; Psalm 90:2; John 1:1

SOAP:
Psalm 90:2

Scripture

WRITE
OUT THE
SCRIPTURE
PASSAGE
FOR THE
DAY.

Observations

WRITE
DOWN 1 OR 2
OBSERVATIONS
FROM THE
PASSAGE.

Applications

WRITE
DOWN 1 OR 2
APPLICATIONS
FROM THE
PASSAGE.

Pray

WRITE OUT
A PRAYER
OVER WHAT
YOU LEARNED
FROM TODAY'S
PASSAGE.

THURSDAY
Scripture for Week 2

Isaiah 44:6-8

6 Thus says the Lord, the King of Israel

    and his Redeemer, the Lord of hosts:

"I am the first and I am the last;

    besides me there is no god.

7 Who is like me? Let him proclaim it.

    Let him declare and set it before me,

since I appointed an ancient people.

    Let them declare what is to come, and what will happen.

8 Fear not, nor be afraid;

    have I not told you from of old and declared it?

    And you are my witnesses!

Is there a God besides me?

    There is no Rock; I know not any."

THURSDAY

READ:
Isaiah 44:6-8

SOAP:
Isaiah 44:6

Scripture

WRITE
OUT THE
SCRIPTURE
PASSAGE
FOR THE
DAY.

Observations

WRITE
DOWN 1 OR 2
OBSERVATIONS
FROM THE
PASSAGE.

Applications

WRITE
DOWN 1 OR 2
APPLICATIONS
FROM THE
PASSAGE.

Pray

WRITE OUT
A PRAYER
OVER WHAT
YOU LEARNED
FROM TODAY'S
PASSAGE.

FRIDAY
Scripture for Week 2

Revelation 21:1-8

1 Then I saw a new heaven and a new earth, for the first heaven and the first earth had passed away, and the sea was no more. 2 And I saw the holy city, new Jerusalem, coming down out of heaven from God, prepared as a bride adorned for her husband. 3 And I heard a loud voice from the throne saying, "Behold, the dwelling place of God is with man. He will dwell with them, and they will be his people, and God himself will be with them as their God. 4 He will wipe away every tear from their eyes, and death shall be no more, neither shall there be mourning, nor crying, nor pain anymore, for the former things have passed away."

5 And he who was seated on the throne said, "Behold, I am making all things new." Also he said, "Write this down, for these words are trustworthy and true." 6 And he said to me, "It is done! I am the Alpha and the Omega, the beginning and the end. To the thirsty I will give from the spring of the water of life without payment. 7 The one who conquers will have this heritage, and I will be his God and he will be my son. 8 But as for the cowardly, the faithless, the detestable, as for murderers, the sexually immoral, sorcerers, idolaters, and all liars, their portion will be in the lake that burns with fire and sulfur, which is the second death."

FRIDAY

READ:
Revelation 21:1-8

SOAP:
Revelation 21:4-8

Scripture

WRITE
OUT THE
SCRIPTURE
PASSAGE
FOR THE
DAY.

Observations

WRITE
DOWN 1 OR 2
OBSERVATIONS
FROM THE
PASSAGE.

Applications

WRITE
DOWN 1 OR 2
APPLICATIONS
FROM THE
PASSAGE.

Pray

WRITE OUT
A PRAYER
OVER WHAT
YOU LEARNED
FROM TODAY'S
PASSAGE.

REFLECTION
QUESTIONS

1. How is Jesus the beginning?

2. List things that have their beginning with Christ.

3. How is Jesus the end?

4. List things that will end when Christ returns.

5. What encouragement do you find in the fact that Jesus is the Alpha and the Omega?

NOTES

WEEK 3

Good Shepherd

He will tend his flock like a shepherd; he will gather the lambs in his arms; he will carry them in his bosom, and gently lead those that are with young.

ISAIAH 40:11

PRAYER

WRITE DOWN YOUR PRAYER REQUESTS
AND PRAISES FOR EACH DAY.

Prayer focus for this week:
Spend time praying for your friends.

MONDAY

TUESDAY

WEDNESDAY

THURSDAY

FRIDAY

CHALLENGE

You can find this listed in our Monday blog post.

MONDAY
Scripture for Week 3

John 10:11-14

11 I am the good shepherd. The good shepherd lays down
his life for the sheep. 12 He who is a hired hand and not
a shepherd, who does not own the sheep, sees the wolf
coming and leaves the sheep and flees, and the wolf snatches
them and scatters them. 13 He flees because he is a hired
hand and cares nothing for the sheep. 14 I am the good
shepherd. I know my own and my own know me,

MONDAY

READ:
John 10:11-14

SOAP:
John 10:11, 14

Scripture

WRITE
OUT THE
SCRIPTURE
PASSAGE
FOR THE
DAY.

Observations

WRITE
DOWN 1 OR 2
OBSERVATIONS
FROM THE
PASSAGE.

Applications

WRITE
DOWN 1 OR 2
APPLICATIONS
FROM THE
PASSAGE.

Pray

WRITE OUT
A PRAYER
OVER WHAT
YOU LEARNED
FROM TODAY'S
PASSAGE.

TUESDAY
Scripture for Week 3

1 Peter 2:24-25

24 He himself bore our sins in his body on the tree, that
we might die to sin and live to righteousness. By his wounds
you have been healed. 25 For you were straying like sheep,
but have now returned to the Shepherd and Overseer of your
souls.

TUESDAY

READ:
1 Peter 2:24-25

SOAP:
1 Peter 2:25

Scripture

WRITE
OUT THE
SCRIPTURE
PASSAGE
FOR THE
DAY.

Observations

WRITE
DOWN 1 OR 2
OBSERVATIONS
FROM THE
PASSAGE.

Applications

WRITE
DOWN 1 OR 2
APPLICATIONS
FROM THE
PASSAGE.

Pray

WRITE OUT
A PRAYER
OVER WHAT
YOU LEARNED
FROM TODAY'S
PASSAGE.

WEDNESDAY

Scripture for Week 3

Psalm 23

1 The Lord is my shepherd; I shall not want.

2   He makes me lie down in green pastures.

He leads me beside still waters.

3   He restores my soul.

He leads me in paths of righteousness

for his name's sake.

4 Even though I walk through the valley of the shadow of

death,

I will fear no evil,

for you are with me;

your rod and your staff,

they comfort me.

5 You prepare a table before me

in the presence of my enemies;

you anoint my head with oil;

my cup overflows.

6 Surely goodness and mercy shall follow me

all the days of my life,

and I shall dwell in the house of the Lord

forever.

WEDNESDAY

READ:
Psalm 23

SOAP:
Psalm 23:1-3

Scripture

WRITE
OUT THE
SCRIPTURE
PASSAGE
FOR THE
DAY.

Observations

WRITE
DOWN 1 OR 2
OBSERVATIONS
FROM THE
PASSAGE.

Applications

WRITE
DOWN 1 OR 2
APPLICATIONS
FROM THE
PASSAGE.

Pray

WRITE OUT
A PRAYER
OVER WHAT
YOU LEARNED
FROM TODAY'S
PASSAGE.

THURSDAY
Scripture for Week 3

Psalm 100

1 Make a joyful noise to the Lord, all the earth!
2   Serve the Lord with gladness!
   Come into his presence with singing!
3 Know that the Lord, he is God!
   It is he who made us, and we are his;
   we are his people, and the sheep of his pasture.
4 Enter his gates with thanksgiving,
   and his courts with praise!
   Give thanks to him; bless his name!
5 For the Lord is good;
   his steadfast love endures forever,
   and his faithfulness to all generations.

THURSDAY

READ:
Psalm 100

SOAP:
Psalm 100:3

Scripture

WRITE
OUT THE
SCRIPTURE
PASSAGE
FOR THE
DAY.

Observations

WRITE
DOWN 1 OR 2
OBSERVATIONS
FROM THE
PASSAGE.

Applications

WRITE
DOWN 1 OR 2
APPLICATIONS
FROM THE
PASSAGE.

Pray

WRITE OUT
A PRAYER
OVER WHAT
YOU LEARNED
FROM TODAY'S
PASSAGE.

FRIDAY

Scripture for Week 3

Luke 2:8-20

8 And in the same region there were shepherds out in the
field, keeping watch over their flock by night. 9 And an angel
of the Lord appeared to them, and the glory of the Lord shone
around them, and they were filled with great fear. 10 And the
angel said to them, "Fear not, for behold, I bring you good
news of great joy that will be for all the people. 11 For unto
you is born this day in the city of David a Savior, who
is Christ the Lord. 12 And this will be a sign for you: you
will find a baby wrapped in swaddling cloths and lying in
a manger." 13 And suddenly there was with the angel a
multitude of the heavenly host praising God and saying,

14 "Glory to God in the highest,
   and on earth peace among those with whom he is pleased!"

15 When the angels went away from them into heaven, the
shepherds said to one another, "Let us go over to Bethlehem
and see this thing that has happened, which the Lord has
made known to us." 16 And they went with haste and found
Mary and Joseph, and the baby lying in a manger. 17 And
when they saw it, they made known the saying that had
been told them concerning this child. 18 And all who heard
it wondered at what the shepherds told them. 19 But Mary
treasured up all these things, pondering them in her
heart. 20 And the shepherds returned, glorifying and praising
God for all they had heard and seen, as it had been told them.

Isaiah 40:11

11 He will tend his flock like a shepherd;
   he will gather the lambs in his arms;
he will carry them in his bosom,
   and gently lead those that are with young.

FRIDAY

READ:
Luke 2:8-20; Isaiah 40:11

SOAP:
Luke 2:8-11; Isaiah 40:11

Scripture

WRITE
OUT THE
SCRIPTURE
PASSAGE
FOR THE
DAY.

Observations

WRITE
DOWN 1 OR 2
OBSERVATIONS
FROM THE
PASSAGE.

Applications

WRITE
DOWN 1 OR 2
APPLICATIONS
FROM THE
PASSAGE.

Pray

WRITE OUT
A PRAYER
OVER WHAT
YOU LEARNED
FROM TODAY'S
PASSAGE.

REFLECTION QUESTIONS

1. What is the job of a shepherd?

2. In what ways is Jesus our Shepherd?

3. What kind of sheep should we be for our Shepherd?

4. What is the "good news of great joy" that the shepherds received?

5. How did the birth of Jesus fulfill that good news?

NOTES

WEEK 4

Prince of Peace

I have said these things to you, that in me you may have peace. In the world you will have tribulation. But take heart; I have overcome the world."

JOHN 16:33

PRAYER

Prayer focus for this week:
Spend time praying for your church.

MONDAY

TUESDAY

WEDNESDAY

THURSDAY

FRIDAY

CHALLENGE

You can find this listed in our Monday blog post.

MONDAY
Scripture for Week 4

Isaiah 9:6-7

6 For to us a child is born,

    to us a son is given;

and the government shall be upon his shoulder,

    and his name shall be called

Wonderful Counselor, Mighty God,

    Everlasting Father, Prince of Peace.

7 Of the increase of his government and of peace

    there will be no end,

on the throne of David and over his kingdom,

    to establish it and to uphold it

with justice and with righteousness

    from this time forth and forevermore.

The zeal of the Lord of hosts will do this.

MONDAY

READ:
Isaiah 9:6-7

SOAP:
Isaiah 9:6

Scripture

WRITE
OUT THE
SCRIPTURE
PASSAGE
FOR THE
DAY.

Observations

WRITE
DOWN 1 OR 2
OBSERVATIONS
FROM THE
PASSAGE.

Applications

WRITE
DOWN 1 OR 2
APPLICATIONS
FROM THE
PASSAGE.

Pray

WRITE OUT
A PRAYER
OVER WHAT
YOU LEARNED
FROM TODAY'S
PASSAGE.

TUESDAY
Scripture for Week 4

John 14:27

27 Peace I leave with you; my peace I give to you. Not as the
world gives do I give to you. Let not your hearts be troubled,
neither let them be afraid.

TUESDAY

READ:
John 14:27

SOAP:
John 14:27

Scripture

WRITE
OUT THE
SCRIPTURE
PASSAGE
FOR THE
DAY.

Observations

WRITE
DOWN 1 OR 2
OBSERVATIONS
FROM THE
PASSAGE.

Applications

WRITE
DOWN 1 OR 2
APPLICATIONS
FROM THE
PASSAGE.

Pray

WRITE OUT
A PRAYER
OVER WHAT
YOU LEARNED
FROM TODAY'S
PASSAGE.

WEDNESDAY
Scripture for Week 4

Colossians 3:15

15 And let the peace of Christ rule in your hearts, to which indeed you were called in one body. And be thankful.

WEDNESDAY

READ:
Colossians 3:15

SOAP:
Colossians 3:15

Scripture

WRITE
OUT THE
SCRIPTURE
PASSAGE
FOR THE
DAY.

Observations

WRITE
DOWN 1 OR 2
OBSERVATIONS
FROM THE
PASSAGE.

Applications

WRITE
DOWN 1 OR 2
APPLICATIONS
FROM THE
PASSAGE.

Pray

WRITE OUT
A PRAYER
OVER WHAT
YOU LEARNED
FROM TODAY'S
PASSAGE.

THURSDAY
Scripture for Week 4

John 16:25-33

25 "I have said these things to you in figures of speech. The hour is coming when I will no longer speak to you in figures of speech but will tell you plainly about the Father. 26 In that day you will ask in my name, and I do not say to you that I will ask the Father on your behalf; 27 for the Father himself loves you, because you have loved me and have believed that I came from God. 28 I came from the Father and have come into the world, and now I am leaving the world and going to the Father."

29 His disciples said, "Ah, now you are speaking plainly and not using figurative speech! 30 Now we know that you know all things and do not need anyone to question you; this is why we believe that you came from God." 31 Jesus answered them, "Do you now believe? 32 Behold, the hour is coming, indeed it has come, when you will be scattered, each to his own home, and will leave me alone. Yet I am not alone, for the Father is with me. 33 I have said these things to you, that in me you may have peace. In the world you will have tribulation. But take heart; I have overcome the world."

THURSDAY

READ:
John 16:25-33

SOAP:
John 16:33

Scripture

WRITE
OUT THE
SCRIPTURE
PASSAGE
FOR THE
DAY.

Observations

WRITE
DOWN 1 OR 2
OBSERVATIONS
FROM THE
PASSAGE.

Applications

WRITE
DOWN 1 OR 2
APPLICATIONS
FROM THE
PASSAGE.

Pray

WRITE OUT
A PRAYER
OVER WHAT
YOU LEARNED
FROM TODAY'S
PASSAGE.

FRIDAY

Scripture for Week 4

Isaiah 53:4-6

4 Surely he has borne our griefs

    and carried our sorrows;

yet we esteemed him stricken,

    smitten by God, and afflicted.

5 But he was pierced for our transgressions;

    he was crushed for our iniquities;

upon him was the chastisement that brought us peace,

    and with his wounds we are healed.

6 All we like sheep have gone astray;

    we have turned—every one—to his own way;

and the Lord has laid on him

    the iniquity of us all.

FRIDAY

READ:
Isaiah 53:4-6

SOAP:
Isaiah 53:5

Scripture

WRITE
OUT THE
SCRIPTURE
PASSAGE
FOR THE
DAY.

Observations

WRITE
DOWN 1 OR 2
OBSERVATIONS
FROM THE
PASSAGE.

Applications

WRITE
DOWN 1 OR 2
APPLICATIONS
FROM THE
PASSAGE.

Pray

WRITE OUT
A PRAYER
OVER WHAT
YOU LEARNED
FROM TODAY'S
PASSAGE.

REFLECTION
QUESTIONS

1. Define Christian peace.

2. What kind of peace does the world want? What kind of peace does the world really need?

3. Where do you need peace?

4. What result should Christ's peace have in our lives?

5. Why is peace something we talk about at Christmas?

NOTES

KNOW THESE TRUTHS
from God's Word

God loves you.

Even when you're feeling unworthy and like the world is stacked against you, God loves you - yes, you - and He has created you for great purpose.

God's Word says, "God so loved the world that He gave His one and only Son, Jesus, that whoever believes in Him shall not perish, but have eternal life" (John 3:16).

Our sin separates us from God.

We are all sinners by nature and by choice, and because of this we are separated from God, who is holy.

God's Word says, "All have sinned and fall short of the glory of God" (Romans 3:23).

Jesus died so that you might have life.

The consequence of sin is death, but your story doesn't have to end there! God's free gift of salvation is available to us because Jesus took the penalty for our sin when He died on the cross.

God's Word says, "For the wages of sin is death, but the free gift of God is eternal life in Christ Jesus our Lord" (Romans 6:23); "God demonstrates His own love toward us, in that while we were yet sinners, Christ died for us" (Romans 5:8).

Jesus lives!

Death could not hold Him, and three days after His body was placed in the tomb Jesus rose again, defeating sin and death forever! He lives today in heaven and is preparing a place in eternity for all who believe in Him.

God's Word says, "In my Father's house are many rooms. If it were not so, would I have told you that I go to prepare a place for you? And if I go and prepare a place for you, I will come again and will take you to myself, that where I am you may be also" (John 14:2-3).

Yes, you can KNOW that you are forgiven.
Accept Jesus as the only way to salvation...

Accepting Jesus as your Savior is not about what you can do, but rather about having faith in what Jesus has already done. It takes recognizing that you are a sinner, believing that Jesus died for your sins, and asking for forgiveness by placing your full trust in Jesus's work on the cross on your behalf.

God's Word says, "If you confess with your mouth that Jesus is Lord and believe in your heart that God raised him from the dead, you will be saved. For with the heart one believes and is justified, and with the mouth one confesses and is saved" (Romans 10:9-10).

Practically, what does that look like?
With a sincere heart, you can pray a simple prayer like this:

God,
I know that I am a sinner.
I don't want to live another day without embracing
the love and forgiveness that You have for me.
I ask for Your forgiveness.
I believe that You died for my sins and rose from the dead.
I surrender all that I am and ask You to be Lord of my life.
Help me to turn from my sin and follow You.
Teach me what it means to walk in freedom as I live under Your grace,
and help me to grow in Your ways as I seek to know You more.
Amen.

If you just prayed this prayer (or something similar in your own words), would you email us at info@lovegodgreatly.com?

We'd love to help get you started on this exciting journey as a child of God!

WELCOME FRIEND

We're so glad you're here

Love God Greatly exists to inspire, encourage, and equip women all over the world to make God's Word a priority in their lives.

INSPIRE

women to make God's Word a priority in their daily lives through our Bible study resources.

ENCOURAGE

women in their daily walks with God through online community and personal accountability.

EQUIP

women to grow in their faith, so that they can effectively reach others for Christ.

Love God Greatly consists of a beautiful community of women who use a variety of technology platforms to keep each other accountable in God's Word.

We start with a simple Bible reading plan, but it doesn't stop there.

Some gather in homes and churches locally, while others connect online with women across the globe. Whatever the method, we lovingly lock arms and unite for this purpose...to Love God Greatly with our lives.

At Love God Greatly, you'll find real, authentic women. Women who are imperfect, yet forgiven. Women who desire less of us, and a whole lot more of Jesus. Women who long to know God through his Word, because we know that Truth transforms and sets us free. Women who are better together, saturated in God's Word and in community with one another.

Love God Greatly is a 501 (C) (3) non-profit organization. Funding for Love God Greatly comes through donations and proceeds from our online Bible study journals and books. LGG is committed to providing quality Bible study materials and believes finances should never get in the way of a woman being able to participate in one of our studies. All journals and translated journals are available to download for free from LoveGodGreatly.com for those who cannot afford to purchase them. Our journals and books are also available for sale on Amazon. Search for "Love God Greatly" to see all of our Bible study journals and books. 100% of proceeds go directly back into supporting Love God Greatly and helping us inspire, encourage and equip women all over the world with God's Word.

THANK YOU for partnering with us!

WHAT WE OFFER:

18 + Translations | Bible Reading Plans | Online Bible Study
Love God Greatly App | 80 + Countries Served
Bible Study Journals & Books | Community Groups

EACH LGG STUDY INCLUDES:

Three Devotional Corresponding Blog Posts
Memory Verses | Weekly Challenge | Weekly Reading Plan
Reflection Questions And More!

OTHER LOVE GOD GREATLY STUDIES INCLUDE:

David | Ecclesiastes | Growing Through Prayer | Names Of God
Galatians | Psalm 119 | 1st & 2nd Peter | Made For Community | Esther
The Road To Christmas | The Source Of Gratitude | You Are Loved

Visit us online at
LOVEGODGREATLY.COM

Made in the USA
Lexington, KY
15 November 2017